Accounting

Accounting made easy, including basic accounting principles, and how to do your own bookkeeping!

Table of Contents

Introduction

Thank you and congratulations on picking up this book, covering the topic of accounting. This book will introduce you to all the basic concepts related to accounting. It is my goal that by the end of this book, you will have a better understanding of the key concepts of accounting, and be able to undertake basic bookkeeping functions.

Most people have a negative view of accounting and accountants in general. Accounting is perceived to be a difficult subject that should only be left to nerdy number-crunchers who have nothing better to do with their time. Nothing could be farther from the truth. Every day we are inundated with all kinds of information, such as home mortgage interest rates, bank balances, and retirement fund statements. If you want to be able to understand financial information and develop your financial literacy skills, you must have some basic knowledge of accounting.

Unfortunately, most people who are interested in developing their accounting skills face immense challenges when searching for good accounting books. A lot of the resource material that is available is simply too complicated for the average reader to understand. Accounting involves a lot of numbers, but most books do not cover the essential theory that should help beginners grasp what these numbers mean. It's as if you have to be a math genius to learn accounting skills.

That is why I decided to write this book. This book offers you something that you cannot find in other accounting texts. I take the time to explain everything in simple and plain English, with technical details and jargon kept to a minimum. I have structured the book in a way that allows you to establish a solid foundation first, before moving on to more challenging topics. This step-by-step approach will help you gain the confidence necessary to tackle more complex accounting challenges ahead.

This book also focuses on topics that non-accountants can easily understand. I have avoided going to deep into topics that only practicing accountants can appreciate. Additionally, I have included illustrations to help you see how every transaction is recorded in the various financial statements used in accounting.

This book is written with a wide audience in mind. You will gain a huge amount of information, whether you are a business manager, entrepreneur, investor, accounting student, practicing bookkeeper, or just someone who wants to take better care of their finances. Regardless of your accounting background, you will benefit from this book.

I begin the book by introducing you to the basics of accounting. You will learn how the accounting process works, its importance, and the four functions of accounting. I also take the time to explain the differences between accounting and bookkeeping. If you have always thought that these two terms mean the same thing, you need to read this book.

Though I make the assumption that you are somewhat familiar with the business world, I take nothing for granted. Therefore, I have also included a chapter that covers some of the most important terminologies used in accounting. This will help you improve your accounting lingo, especially when you start learning how to prepare the financial statements.

The book covers key bookkeeping concepts such as the accounting equation, the double entry rule, cash-based accounting, and accrual accounting. These are extremely important topics, so make sure you master these concepts before you move on the balance sheet, income statement, and cash flow statement. With all this knowledge in the back of your mind, you will find it a lot easier to tackle the final chapter on financial ratios.

I can tell you from personal experience that there is no need to fear this topic. I too had to overcome all the preconceptions and myths regarding accounting, but once I began studying and mastering the fundamentals, everything started making sense. I can assure you that once you have finished reading this book, you will no longer struggle to understand accounting concepts. Everything you will learn here will enhance your confidence in handling more advanced accounting techniques and calculations.

I can promise you that with this book, you will quickly learn the basics of accounting. You will realize that accounting is not that difficult if you grasp a few key concepts and practice them on a regular basis.

Are you ready?

Let's get started...

Chapter 1: The Basics Of Accounting

In this chapter, you will learn the basic structure of accounting. You will learn how to define accounting, its relevance to you, and why it is different from bookkeeping. I will also talk about some of the preconceptions regarding accounting. By the end of this chapter, you will have a firm understanding of what accounting is and how it affects the different aspects of your life.

What Is Accounting?

The formal definition that is usually given to accounting is this:

In simpler terms, we can define accounting as a standardized system that is used to measure financial performance by recording and organizing transactions. This system helps you to evaluate your past performance, current condition, and future prospects.

Many people think that accounting is just for business and organizations, but that is not true. Accounting principles are necessary for anyone who wants to become financially literate. It is the language of finance, taxes, business, and investing.

Now that you have an idea of what accounting is, let's break it down further so that you can understand how the different accounting functions work together.

How Accounting Works

Accounting generally consists of four functions:

• Recording

• Organizing

• Summarizing

• Evaluating and interpreting results of financial activities

However, before you can actually record anything, you must first have something to record. In accounting, we usually record a transaction or any event that has a financial impact on you. This transaction is always represented in the form of a document. In accounting, we do not record conversations or ideas. If you do not have a document to back up a transaction, it cannot be recorded.

If you are running a business, you may find that there are a lot of documents that must be recorded, and therefore, there has to be a logical system to do this. This is where the journal comes in. A journal is simply a record of all the transactions you have engaged in, listed in chronological order.

Once you begin to record your transactions in a journal, you will quickly accumulate a large volume of data. This data is then grouped together according to the nature of the transaction. For example, all the money coming in is separated from any money that is paid out.

But what do you do with all this data? Anyone who looks at your journal will only see a bunch of figures associated with different transactions. This raw data needs to make more sense.

Therefore, the next step is to summarize the data in a meaningful way. The summaries generated from the journal records must be able to answer specific questions, such as:

• How much money did I make from sales this month?

• What were my total expenses last month?

• What types of expenses cost me the most money?

• How much do I owe?

• How much money is owed to me?

• How much money do I have in cash?

As you can see, all the different transactions recorded in the journal are now beginning to provide meaningful information. But this information is still not helpful unless it is acted upon.

These records must be reported to the manager of the business in a format that is easy to understand. The accountant must evaluate and interpret the impact the information has on the business. This is usually done by preparing a financial statement, for example, a balance sheet or income statement.

It is important to note that every business can create its own unique way of keeping its accounting books. However, all accounting systems must have the following features:

1. Every transaction must be supported by a business document. If goods or services are sold, an item is purchased, a contract is signed, or any similar financial event occurs, there has to be a document to represent the transaction.

2. There must be different journals to record and classify the details in the documents.

3. There must be different ledgers to summarize the journal entries.

4. Financial reports must be prepared to present the summarized information.

There may be slight variations in the above features depending on the type of business and the way transactions are processed. But the important thing is to have a solid understanding of the fundamentals of the accounting process. This will enable you to handle any accounting problem you face.

Importance Of Learning Accounting

There are many reasons why you need to learn some accounting. While there are some people who have a negative view of accounting, I guarantee you that you still use some form of accounting function in your everyday life.

For example, in many homes, the mother is the chief accountant. She records every major household expense and the payments made. She prepares a monthly budget at the beginning of every month and even keeps receipts in a small folder somewhere. You may not realize it, but these are all basic accounting functions that are used on a small scale to manage personal finances.

However, I would like to talk about the two major reasons for learning basic accounting. The first reason is to understand the terminology and valuation methods used. Every day, we are inundated with tons of accounting-generated data. A lot of this data just passes us by because we do not know how to make intelligent use of this information. But how do you expect to play the financial game when you don't know how the score is kept?

The second reason for knowing accounting basics is to defend your interests. There are a lot of people out there in the financial world who make a living fleecing people who are ignorant about accounting. There are individuals and organizations who will give you bad accounting advice as long as it benefits their bottom line. The best way to defend yourself is to have some basic accounting knowledge that enables you to grasp the critical points and ask the right questions.

Preconceptions And Stereotypes About Accounting

There are a number of preconceptions that you may have about accounting. You are not alone. The majority of people perceive accounting to be a tedious practice that is only done by a bunch of boring and colorless individuals called accountants. However, most of these myths are way off the mark. Here are some of the biggest preconceptions about accounting:

1. You have to be a math genius to understand accounting – While it is true that accounting is all about numbers, it doesn't mean that you have to be a math whizz to do some basic accounting. You just need to know arithmetic. There is no calculus or algebraic equations to deal with. This preconception is usually perpetuated by those who are simply scared of anything that has to do with numbers.

2. You don't need to know accounting if you have accounting software – Most business owners tend to believe that they can use accounting software to replace an accountant. While the software we currently have is very advanced and quite useful, it cannot replace the expertise of a qualified accountant. There are certain unquantifiable circumstances and complexities that technology cannot account for when developing financial strategies. Accounting software may enhance your ability to perform accounting functions, but you still need some basic accounting skills to make sure you do everything right.

3. My business is doing well, so I don't need accounting – When clients are pouring into your business and the money is flowing, it is easy to forget the need to prepare accounting reports. However, when things start to deteriorate, you will quickly realize the folly of your ways. By learning some basic accounting, you will be able to know the health of your business and how to make the right adjustments when your finances are not in good shape.

4. Accountants are too detail-oriented – I don't know why people see this as a bad thing. The truth is that a good accountant will always look at the fine details and how they fit into the grand scheme of things. When doing your accounts, you don't have a choice of whether to look at all the details or not. It is a necessity.

Accounting Versus Bookkeeping

These are two terms that are commonly used interchangeably, yet they mean totally different things. Most people assume that accountants and bookkeepers perform the same function, but as you are about to find out, that is not the case. There are major differences between accounting and bookkeeping.

Accounting refers to a much wider concept than bookkeeping. When we talk about accounting, we encompass the entire process of summarizing, interpreting, and relaying information about the financial impact of an activity. The management of a business can take a look at the data provided by an accountant and use it to make a business decision. This is because accounting is focused on gauging the financial situation and relaying that information to the people in charge. Accounting is more complex and analytical than bookkeeping, so you must have special skills to become an accountant.

Bookkeeping refers to the process of collecting, organizing, and storing the financial records of an entity. This is what most individuals and small businesses do when they want to track their finances. Bookkeeping does not involve the evaluation, interpretation, and preparation of any financial statements. Therefore, it is difficult for you to make a good business decision based on bookkeeping data alone. A bookkeeper doesn't need any special skills because they are simply noting down transactions in a journal.

On the other hand, we are beginning to see the merging of some accounting and bookkeeping functions. Some of the bookkeeping software we have today has incorporated certain accounting functions. For example, some bookkeeping technology is now able to create financial statements.

I will talk more about basic bookkeeping in Chapter 3 of this book.

Chapter Summary

Here are the key points of the chapter:

• Accounting is a standardized process of recording, classifying, summarizing, and interpreting transactions to determine the financial performance of an entity.

• There are two main reasons for learning basic accounting. The first is that you need to be able to utilize all the accounting information we are bombarded with daily. Secondly, accounting knowledge will help you avoid being conned by shrewd financial advisors.

• There are many preconceptions and stereotypes about accounting, such as, "You must be a math genius to understand accounting" or, "Software can replace accountants", "Only failing business owners need to learn accounting skills" and "Accountants are too obsessed with details".

• Accounting and bookkeeping serve two different purposes. While bookkeeping involves collecting and storing financial records, accounting involves analyzing and interpreting those records to improve the decision-making process.

In the next chapter, you will learn some of the key terminologies linked to accounting practices.

Chapter 2: Understanding Accounting Terminology

In this chapter, you will learn the vocabulary that is used in accounting. It is important that you have a firm grasp of these terms because you will be coming across some of them later on in this book.

Accounts

An account is simply a record of a specific piece of accounting information. Think of it this way: An account is to an accounting system what a folder is to a filing cabinet. Therefore, you have one filing cabinet with several folders containing topics such as bank loans, utility bills, employee wages, cash, and etc. You cannot take your utility bills records and file them in the employee wages account. Each account must contain its own specific records.

Another thing you should note is that every account generates a monetary value that helps us to categorize it accordingly. We generally categorize accounts as Assets, Liabilities, Expenses, and Income. For example, at the end of the month, you will owe $X to your utility company and $Y in the form of employee wages. These two accounts will fall under the Expense account, the bank loan will fall under the Liabilities account, and the cash in hand will be placed under Assets.

Assets

This is a physical item or intangible right that has economic value to the owner. Examples of assets include cash, merchandise, tools and equipment, buildings, accounts receivable, and inventory for sale. The term 'Accounts Receivable' refers to a promise that a client makes to pay later for goods or services that they have already received.

When listing assets on a balance sheet, we usually arrange them according to how easy it is to convert them into cash. There are three groups of assets:

1. Current assets – These are assets that can be sold, converted into cash, or used up in less than a year. In other words, it is expected that a current asset will provide an economic benefit for less than 12 months. Examples include:

• Cash – The money you have in your savings and checking account.

• Debtors – Money owed to the business.

• Securities – Investments such as stocks and bonds.

• Inventories – Merchandise for sale or raw materials.

• Accounts Receivables – The money customers owe you.

• Notes Receivables – Promissory notes issued by customers to pay you a specific amount plus interest by a specific date.

• Prepaid Expenses – Services or supplies you have paid for but are not using yet, such as prepaid insurance.

2. Fixed assets – These are tangible, long-lasting resources that the business uses and are not for sale. Fixed assets are expected to keep generating economic benefits for longer than 12 months. For example:

• Land

• Buildings

• Furniture and fixtures

• Vehicles

• Machinery and equipment

3. Intangible assets – These are non-physical assets whose value can be sold or licensed to another entity, for example:

• Goodwill – This will only appear in financial records when the business is being sold. It represents the value of a company's reputation among its customers.

• Patents

• Copyrights

• Trademarks

Liabilities

This is a legal commitment that a business has to pay a debt. This debt can be paid in cash or with goods and services. There are two categories of liabilities. These are:

1. Current liabilities – These are liabilities that must be paid within a short period of time, usually 12 months. They are usually paid off using the existing current assets. Examples include:

• Accounts Payable – This is an unwritten promise to pay your lenders or suppliers a specific amount of money at a specific future date. Think of it as the reverse counterpart of Accounts Receivable. It is one of the most common forms of current liabilities.

• Notes Payable – This is a written promise to pay back your lenders a specified sum plus interest by a specific date. Think of it as the reverse counterpart of Notes Receivable. It is also one of the most common forms of current liabilities.

• Accrued Expenses – These are expenses that are incurred but will be paid for in the near future, for example; wages, taxes, and interest.

2. Long-term liabilities – These are liabilities that can be paid off after a long period of time. It is generally accepted that long-

term liabilities should only be paid after one year has lapsed. Examples include:

• Mortgage Note Payable

• Bonds Payable

• Any other long-term debts

It is important to note that there are some instances where long-term liabilities are classified as current liabilities. For example, if you have a mortgage and an installment is due within the first year, this initial payment will appear as a current liability on your balance sheet. The remainder of the installments will then be considered long-term liabilities.

Capital

This refers to your net worth. It is the money available to you after you have paid off all your creditors. If your business does not have any liabilities, then your capital or owner's equity will be equivalent to the value of the business assets.

The Business Entity Concept

This is an accounting principle that separates a business entity from the people involved in the business. When you are preparing accounting reports, you must focus on the transactions relating to the business, and not the owners or employees.

Revenue

This is the income you receive when you engage in regular business activities like selling goods and services. It can also include royalties, interest received, or dividends.

Costs

This is also referred to as Cost of Goods Sold. It is the amount of money spent on buying or manufacturing goods for selling.

Expenses

This is the money a company spends to ensure operations run smoothly, for example; salaries and wages. Expenses are not directly related to goods or services.

Net Income

This is also known as net profit. It is the money that remains after you have deducted all your expenses from your earnings.

Invoices

These are documents that are sent to a client or customer to request payment for products or services provided.

Ledger

This is a collection of financial information that is related to one another. For example, expenditures, accounts payable, revenues, and accounts receivable ledgers.

Owner's Equity

This is the value that remains once a business has met all its liabilities. It can also be defined as the money left over for the owner after deducting liabilities from company assets. Since the company and its owner are considered to be distinct entities, owner's equity is actually the money the business owes the owner.

Chapter Summary

Here are the key points of the chapter:

• An account is a record of a specific piece of accounting information. The four categories of accounts are Assets, Liabilities, Expenses, and Income.

• An asset is a physical item or intangible right that has economic value to the owner. The three types of assets include Current, Fixed, and Intangible Assets.

• A liability is a legal commitment to pay a debt. The two types of liabilities are Current, and Long-Term Liabilities.

• Capital is equivalent to Assets minus Liabilities.

• The Business Entity Concept is a principle that separates a business entity from the owners and employees when preparing accounting reports.

• A ledger is a collection of related financial information.

• Owner's Equity is the value that remains once a business has met all its liabilities.

In the next chapter, you will learn the basic bookkeeping concepts.

Chapter 3: Basic Bookkeeping Concepts

In this chapter, you will learn about two very important concepts of bookkeeping, namely the accounting equation and double-entry bookkeeping. These two concepts lie at the center of the whole accounting process. Once you have understood how they work, you will find it much easier to handle any financial report or statement. This chapter also explains the difference between the cash and accrual accounting system when setting up a bookkeeping system.

But first, let's look at a brief history of bookkeeping.

History of Bookkeeping

Bookkeeping, as it is currently used globally, was developed by Luca Pacioli in 1424. Pacioli, who was one of the associates of Leonardo da Vinci, wrote the first bookkeeping guide and is thus regarded as the father of bookkeeping. Prior to this, Benedetto Corugli had written a book explaining how to use the double-entry method when recording financial transactions.

Double-entry bookkeeping became more popular than single-entry bookkeeping because it provided more built-in controls and was thus more accurate. Initially, all financial transactions were manually recorded in ledger accounts. This required a high level of care and effort. However, bookkeeping has become more systematic and automatic thanks to advancements in computer technologies.

The Accounting Equation

In the previous chapter, we defined the terms 'liability' and 'owner's equity'. These two components have one thing in common – they are both regarded as equities. Equities are the claims made on the assets of a business. External parties can make a claim on the assets of a business through its liabilities, while the owner does the same through owner's equity.

This special relationship between assets, liabilities, and owner's equity can be represented in the form of an equation. This equation is known as the accounting equation, and is described as follows:

This may seem like a very simple equation, but the accounting equation practically defines all aspects of the accounting process. It doesn't matter whether you are running a small business or a multinational corporation. As long as you are running an entity that is legally required to prepare financial reports, your transactions are subject to the accounting equation.

The accounting equation establishes one fundamental rule: It must always balance!

In other words, the total value of assets must always be equal to the liabilities plus owner's equity. There are no special conditions whatsoever where this equation is allowed to be out of balance.

We all know that when you are starting a business, you have to put down some of your own money to finance operations. At that moment, the value of your assets is equal to your equity because there are no liabilities yet. When you get a bank loan, the value of your company's liabilities goes up. The value of your assets must also increase by the same amount as the loan. Therefore, the accounting equation will still balance.

For example, if a company has assets worth $200,000 and liabilities valued at $135,000, the owner's equity must be whatever is left over. That is $65,000. There is no way that the owner's equity can be larger than this because there wouldn't be enough assets to pay the owner. On the other hand, the owner's equity cannot be less than $65,000. If the owner only claimed $55,000, who would claim the remaining amount? The creditors are not entitled to the leftover $10,000. Only the owner can claim it, therefore, the owner's equity must be the full $65,000.

It is important to note that when a business is closing down, the company's liabilities must be taken care of first before the owner can claim any of the assets. The creditors will get their share of the assets and whatever remains belongs to the owner of the business.

The Double-Entry System

This is an accounting principle where every transaction must involve two accounts, and therefore, must have two corresponding entries in the financial records.

For example, if a company borrows money from a bank, the Cash account of the company will increase, while the Loans Payable account will also show a corresponding increase. If the company then uses the money for advertising, the Advertising Expense account will decrease, while the Cash account will also decrease. As you can see, this single transaction will create two entries.

The double-entry system also supports the accounting equation we discussed earlier. Remember that assets must always be equal to liabilities plus owner's equity.

Let's say the company above has assets worth $10,000 with no liabilities. This means the assets are equal to the owner's equity. If the company gets a $5,000 loan from a bank, the assets and liabilities of the company both increase by $5,000. However, the owner's equity stays the same.

Let's say the company then decides to use $7,000 for advertising expenses. Since this is cash going out, the company's assets will decrease. If the accounting equation is to balance out, then either the liabilities or owner's equity must also reduce by $7,000. The bank loan is a fixed amount, and the bank doesn't really care where the money went as long as the company pays back the loan. Therefore, liabilities cannot reduce. This means that owner's equity will reduce from $10,000 to $3,000. Therefore, the accounting equation will balance out.

Another aspect of the double-entry system is that for every amount that is recorded on the debit side of the general ledger, there will be an equal amount entered on the credit side. Even simple transactions must have a debit and a credit entry. A debit usually refers to how the money is used while credit refers to the source of the money.

For example, if a company gives an employee a $500 payroll check, the transaction will be entered as a credit in the Cash in Bank account, while the same amount will be debited from the Payroll Expense account.

Advantages Of The Double-Entry System

The double-entry system has the following benefits:

1. Scientific – This is a scientific way of accounting because it operates on specific rules and principles. Every financial transaction must have two entries.

2. Systematic – Financial transactions are recorded chronologically with the appropriate narration for each entry.

3. Control – Due to the fact that detailed records are kept through the double entry system, it becomes easier to glean the information necessary for cost control.

4. Accuracy – Since every transaction produces both a debit and credit record, there is arithmetical accuracy when the financial reports are tallied.

5. Profit or loss – It helps to verify whether a company has made a true profit or a loss when preparing the Profit and Loss Account.

6. Financial position – It reveals the financial health of a business when the Balance Sheet statement is prepared.

Cash Versus Accrual Accounting Systems

When you are establishing a bookkeeping system, you will have to consider whether to use a cash-based system or an accrual accounting system. These are two methods of tracking accounting records.

Cash-based accounting is probably what you use when tracking your personal finances. In cash-based accounting, you only record revenue when you receive the money, while expenses are only recorded when you pay out money. For example, if you sell some merchandise on credit and expect to be paid in 30 days, you will only record the transaction when the client pays you the cash. The same applies when you purchase inventory on credit. Small businesses usually prefer cash-based accounting.

If you are running a sole-proprietorship business, whether it's from your home or in a small office, you are better off setting up a cash accounting system. This will be more convenient because you will be dealing with a lot of cash transactions. Most small businesses start with the cash accounting system and adopt the accrual system as they grow larger.

The accrual system is more convenient for businesses that intend to sell on credit, or buy merchandise from suppliers on credit. In this system, you record a transaction according to the accounting period it was earned or incurred. For example, if you sell merchandise today on credit, you will record the transaction immediately, even if the customer will pay you 30 days later. This method is mostly used by large companies.

Chapter Summary

Here are the key points of the chapter:

• The accounting equation states that assets must be equal to liabilities plus owner's equity.

• The accounting equation defines all aspects of the accounting process, and every financial report is subject to it. The equation must always balance.

• The double-entry system is an accounting principle where every transaction must involve two accounts and must have two corresponding entries in the financial records.

• The double-entry system is used to balance the accounting equation.

• In the double-entry system, every amount recorded on the debit side of the ledger will have an equal amount entered on the credit side.

• A debit usually refers to how the money is used while credit refers to the source of the money.

• There are two ways to track your accounting records. These are cash-based accounting and the accrual method.

• In cash-based accounting, you record revenue and expenses when you receive and pay out money respectively.

• In accrual accounting, you only record a transaction according to the accounting period it was earned or incurred.

In the next chapter, you will learn about the balance sheet.

Chapter 4: The Balance Sheet

In this chapter, you will be introduced to the balance sheet and learn how the accounting equation is fundamental to this particular financial report. You will learn how to prepare a balance sheet, classify the information it contains, and record transactions using the double entry system.

What Is A Balance Sheet?

This is an accounting report that shows the financial condition of a company at a specific point in time by detailing its assets, liabilities, and equity. In a balance sheet, the assets are usually listed on one side, while the liabilities and owner's equity are totaled on the other. It follows the same principle as the accounting equation, as shown below.

Assets	=	Liabilities	+	Owner's Equity

Assets	Liabilities plus Owner's Equity
TOTAL ASSETS	TOTAL EQUITIES

Now let's look at an example of a simple balance sheet belonging to a company called Fabulous Hair. For now, I want you to focus on the type of information that is entered and the overall structure of the balance sheet. Later on, we will look at how different accounts are classified and arranged within the balance sheet.

Fabulous Hair
Balance Sheet as at 31 December 2017

ASSETS			LIABILITIES		
Assets			**Liabilities**		
Cash at Bank		$5,000	Creditors		$8,000
Debtors		$5,000	Bank Loan		$15,000
Stock of Hair Dye		$10,000	**Owner's Equity**		
Furniture and Fixtures		$15,000	Capital - Adrian		$12,000
Total Assets		**$35,000**	**Total Liabilities**		**$35,000**

The first thing you need to notice is the title of the report. You must indicate the name of the entity the report is prepared for (Fabulous Hair), the type of report (balance sheet), and the date at which the report is accurate (31 December 2017). It is extremely critical that you always indicate this date because a balance sheet can only be accurate on the day that you prepare it. By 1st of January 2018, the assets and liabilities could be different, meaning a new balance sheet will have to be prepared.

If you look at the headings inside the balance sheet, you will notice that they represent the elements of the accounting equation. The individual accounts are then placed under these headings. As you can see, capital is listed under owner's equity, with the name of the owner also indicated. If the business makes any profits, they will also be placed under owner's equity.

Classification Of Balance Sheet Items

One of the main purposes of accounting is to provide financial information for making better decisions. Therefore, accounting professionals are always looking for ways to make this information more useful for decision-makers. One simple and effective way of achieving this is by grouping together particular items that share common characteristics.

Fabulous Hair
Balance Sheet as at 31 December 2017

ASSETS			LIABILITIES		
Current Assets			**Current Liabilities**		
Cash at Bank		$5,000	Creditors		$8,000
Debtors		$5,000	Loan - ABC Bank		$5,000
Stock of Hair Dye		$10,000			
	Total Current Assets	$20,000		Total Current Liabilities	$13,000
Fixed Assets			**Long-term Liabilities**		
Furniture and fixtures		$15,000	Loan - ABC Bank		$10,000
	Total Net Fixed Assets	$15,000		Total Long-Term Liabilities	$10,000
			Owner's Equity		
			Capital - Adrian		$12,000
				Total Owner's Equity	$12,000
TOTAL ASSETS		$35,000	**TOTAL LIABILITIES AND EQUITY**		$35,000

In the balance sheet above, you can see that there are two major classes of information - assets, and liabilities. However, it is possible to group the individual items further. For example, under assets, we can have current assets and fixed assets. Under liabilities, we can have current liabilities and long-term liabilities.

By classifying the existing information even further, we enhance the quality of the information, thus allowing better analysis and decision-making.

In the example, the bank loan that was originally presented as $15,000 has now been split into two. When explaining the difference between current and long-term liabilities in Chapter 2, I stated that there are times when an item such as a bank loan can be both a long-term as well as current liability. This happens if the bank expects the first installment to be paid within 12 months. This is why the balance sheet shows the first installment of $5,000 as a current liability while the remaining $10,000 is recorded as a long-term liability.

Recording Double Entry Transactions

We have seen how the accounting equation affects the balance sheet. However, the rules of double-entry also apply when recording transactions on a balance sheet. Every transaction will produce at least two entries that will affect the accounting equation, but the equation must still balance. Consider the example below:

Mike has decided to start a pool cleaning service. On January 1, 2018, he contributes $12,000 cash to start the business as Mike's Pool Cleaners.

Due to this transaction, Mike's company now has $12,000 in its bank account. On top of that, because the money was contributed by the owner (who is legally considered to be a separate entity), owner's equity increases by $12,000.

According to the accounting equation:

Assets	=	Liabilities	+	Owner's Equity
Bank $12,000				Capital $12,000

So, how will this information be represented in a balance sheet according to the double entry principle?

MIKE'S POOL CLEANERS
Balance Sheet as at 1st January 2018

ASSETS		LIABILITIES	
Assets		**Liabilities**	
Cash at Bank	$12,000	Nil	
		Owner's Equity	
		Capital - Mike	$12,000
Total Assets	$12,000	**Total Liabilities and Equity**	$12,000

The transaction has had a positive effect on two items – Bank and Capital. Both have increased by $12,000 and the accounting equation is still balanced.

Let's say that on the next day, the company decides to purchase a pickup truck on credit from Pete's Trucks for $20,000. How will the accounting equation be affected?

Assets	=	Liabilities	+	Owner's Equity
Truck $20,000		Creditor – Pete's Trucks $20,000		

This time, the cash in the bank is not affected but a different asset called Truck is added. On the other side of the equation, a liability called Creditor is created. This represents the amount of money owed to Pete's Trucks.

The balance sheet will also change as shown below:

MIKE'S POOL CLEANERS
Balance Sheet as at 2nd January 2018

ASSETS		LIABILITIES	
Assets		**Liabilities**	
Cash at Bank	$12,000	Creditor	$20,000
Truck	$20,000	**Owner's Equity**	
		Capital - Mike	$12,000
Total Assets	$32,000	**Total Liabilities and Equity**	$32,000

Let's add one more transaction to drive the point home. On January 3rd, 2018, the company purchases new cleaning equipment worth $5,000. How will this impact the accounting equation and balance sheet?

Assets	=	Liabilities	+	Owner's Equity
↓Bank $5,000				
↑Cleaning Equipment $5,000				

The effect on the balance sheet would be:

MIKE'S POOL CLEANERS
Balance Sheet as at 3rd January 2018

ASSETS		LIABILITIES	
Assets		**Liabilities**	
Cash at Bank	$7,000	Creditor	$20,000
Truck	$20,000	**Owner's Equity**	
Cleaning Equipment	$5,000	Capital - Mike	$12,000
Total Assets	**$32,000**	**Total Liabilities and Equity**	**$32,000**

This transaction increases the number of assets but reduces the amount of money in the bank. This means that there is no overall change in the total value of the assets. This proves that the accounting equation and balance sheet can still balance even when a transaction only affects items on one side of the equation.

The bottom line is that every transaction will have a dual effect on the accounting equation, and if you record these effects correctly, the equation will balance. However, if the totals in the balance sheet do not tally, then it is likely that you made a mistake in the way you recorded the transaction.

Chapter Summary

Here are the key points of the chapter:

• A balance sheet is an accounting report that shows the financial condition of a company at a specific point in time by detailing its assets, liabilities, and equity.

• Every balance sheet must indicate the name of the entity the report is prepared for, the type of report, and the date at which the report is accurate.

• In a balance sheet, there are two major classes of information - assets and liabilities. However, these classes can be broken down further into current assets, fixed assets, current liabilities, and long-term liabilities.

• Classification enhances the quality of the information, thus allowing for better analysis and decision-making.

• The accounting equation and double entry principle are at the core of every transaction recorded on the balance sheet. The totals of the balance sheet must always balance out. If they do not, then there is an error in the recording.

In the next chapter, you will learn about the income statement.

Chapter 5: The Income Statement

In this chapter, you will learn about the income statement, which is also known as the profit and loss statement. By the end of this chapter, you will be able to create a basic income statement and identify all the accounts that need to be recorded on an income statement.

What Is The Income Statement?

This is a report that shows the financial performance of a company during a particular accounting period. The income statement is an important financial statement because it indicates the profitability of the company on a monthly, quarterly, or yearly basis. It provides a summary of all the revenues a company has earned and then deducts the expenses incurred to generate either the net profit or net loss for that accounting period.

But, why is this financial report so important?

There are several reasons why people are interested in the profitability of a company. If a business is operating on a net loss, there will be very few creditors or lenders who will be willing to extend more credit to the company. However, if the income statement shows a net profit, then this will be proof that the company is able to utilize borrowed funds effectively. Apart from lenders and creditors, there are other groups of people who are also interested in the ability of a company to operate profitably. These include potential investors, competitors, labor unions, company management, and government agencies.

Though an income statement can take on many different formats depending on the complexity of a company's business activities, there are particular components that are part and parcel of this financial report. These are revenues, gains, expenses, and losses. An income statement never includes any cash payments or cash receipts.

The basic premise of an income statement is simple. If deducting the total expenses and losses from the total revenues and gains generates a positive value, then the company has made a net profit. However, if the bottom line is negative, then the company has made a net loss.

Revenues and Gains

Revenues and gains usually appear in three forms:

1. Revenues from primary activities.

These are also known as operating revenues. If you are dealing with a retailer, manufacturer, or wholesaler, the operating revenues are called sales, or sales revenues. On the other hand, if a company provides services to clients, its revenues will be referred to as fees earned, or service revenues.

One thing you should note is that the income statement rarely corresponds to the actual cash flow of the company. Every company wants to boost its cash flow, but not all companies go out of their way to increase their reported earnings. This is usually done in an attempt to lower taxes.

In Chapter 3, you learned about cash accounting versus accrual accounting. The reason why the income statement seldom matches cash flow is that the majority of companies choose to use accrual accounting instead of cash accounting. In accrual accounting, revenues are reported when the actual sale is made, even if the client pays 30 days later. Likewise, expenses are reported when they are incurred, even though actual payment hasn't been made.

In other words, there is a distinction between revenues and receipts. By understanding the difference between the two, you can ensure that you always report the revenues from a transaction one time.

2. Revenues from secondary activities.

These are known as non-operating revenues. They are revenues earned from activities that are not tied to buying or selling inventory or services. For example, a company may earn some interest from its cash in the bank, or by renting out some vacant space. These revenues are usually recorded separately on the income statement from those earned from primary activities.

3. Gains.

Gains are earned from transactions that are outside the main economic activities of the business. For example, if a company sells one of its cars for $8,000 and the asset had depreciated over the years to a book value of $5,500, the gain that would be reported in the income statement would be $2,500. Gains are usually reported in the accounting period when the asset was disposed of.

Expenses and Losses

There are three forms of expenses and losses:

1. Expenses from primary activities.

These are the expenses a business incurs when trying to earn regular operating revenues, for example; sales commissions, utilities, employee wages and bonuses, and etc. The accrual accounting system is also used here, which means that the expenses are not reported at the same time as when the cash payment is made.

2. Expenses from secondary activities.

These are also known as non-operating expenses and do not involve the buying and selling function of the business. A good example would be Interest Expense.

3. Losses.

These are losses made when long-term assets are sold. For
example, if a company sells one of its cars for $5,000 and the
book value is $6,500, the loss that would be reported in the
income statement would be $1,500. Losses are usually reported
in the accounting period when the asset was disposed of.

The Single-Step Income Statement

This is the simplest version of an income statement. There is
only a single subtraction involved when calculating net income.

Here is a condensed version of an income statement:

Random Products Ltd.
Income Statement
For the Three Months Ended March 31, 2018

Revenues & Gains	$50,000
Expenses & Losses	$29,000
Net Income	**$21,000**

Just like in the balance sheet, the title of the income statement is
extremely critical. The first thing that appears is the name of the
company followed by the words 'Income Statement'. After that,
there is the accounting period in which the transactions
occurred. Income statements can be prepared for any time
period, therefore, you must always tell the reader the exact
period that the report covers. For example, an income statement
can indicate time periods such as 'Year Ended March 31', 'Month
Ended March 31', 'Quarter Ended March 31', or 'Five Weeks
Ended March 31'.

Here is a sample of a more detailed single-step income statement:

Random Products Ltd.
Income Statement
For the Three Months Ended March 31, 2018

Revenues & Gains	
Sales revenues	$45,000
Interest on revenues	$3,000
Gain on sale of asset	$2,000
Total revenue & gains	**$50,000**
Expenses & Losses	
Cost of goods sold	$20,000
Commissions expense	$5,000
Advertizing expense	$2,000
Loss from lawsuit	$2,000
Total expenses and losses	**$29,000**
Net Income	**$21,000**

Multiple-Step Income Statement

This is an income statement format where multiple subtractions are done when calculating the net income. The reason why there are more steps in this format is that the operating revenues and gains are separated from the non-operating revenues and gains. This also applies to the expenses and losses. Unlike the single-step income statement, the multiple-step income statement shows the gross profit.

Here is a sample of a multiple-step income statement:

Random Products Ltd.
Income Statement
For the Three Months Ended March 31, 2018

Sales		$45,000
Cost of goods sold		$20,000
Gross profit		$25,000
Operating expenses		
Selling expenses		
Commissions expense	$5,000	
Advertizing expense	$2,000	$7,000
Total operating expenses		$7,000
Operating income		$18,000
Non-operating or other		
Interest on revenues		$3,000
Gain on sale of asset		$2,000
Loss from lawsuit		$ (2,000)
Total non-operating		$3,000
Net Income		$21,000

From the above income statement, you can see that there are three steps involved in arriving at the net income. These are:

• Subtracting the cost of goods sold from net sales to determine the gross profit.

• Subtracting the total operating expenses from the gross profit to determine the operating income.

• Adding the operating income to the total non-operating revenues, gains, and losses to determine the net income.

The loss from the lawsuit is placed in brackets to indicate that it is to be subtracted from the other non-operating items.

Using the multiple-step income statement has two advantages:

1. It clearly shows you the gross profit. Most of the people who read financial statements look at a company's gross profit and compare it to previous gross margins. Readers also compare it to other companies within the industry.

2. It shows you the operating income, which represents the profit the company made from its primary buying and selling activities.

Chapter Summary

Here are the key points of the chapter:

• The income statement is a report that shows the financial performance of a company during a particular accounting period. It indicates the profitability of the company on a monthly, quarterly, or yearly basis.

• An income statement must show revenues, gains, expenses, and losses. However, cash payments and cash receipts are not to be included.

• The Single-Step income statement is the simplest version of an income statement. It only involves one subtraction when calculating net income.

• The name of the company, the title of the financial report and the time period for which the report is prepared must all be stated at the top of the income statement.

• The multiple-step income statement involves multiple subtractions when calculating the net income. The operating revenues, gains, expenses, and losses are separated from the non-operating revenues, gains, expenses, and losses.

• Unlike the single-step income statement, the multiple-step income statement shows the gross profit and subtotal operating income.

In the next chapter, you will learn about the cash flow statement.

Chapter 6: Cash Flow Statement

In this chapter, you will learn what a cash flow statement is, its uses, and how it is prepared. You will also learn how changes that occur in the balance sheet affect the cash flow statement.

What Is A Cash Flow Statement?

This is a financial report that records all the cash generated and used by a company during a specific time interval. This time interval covered is picked by the company, and is always stated clearly in the heading of the cash flow statement. The cash flow statement is officially referred to as the statement of cash flows.

Uses Of The Cash Flow Statement

Savvy investors and business people use the cash flow statement to get particular information. Here are two things this financial statement can tell us:

1. The net income can be compared to the cash from the operating activities. If the amount of cash is always higher than the net income, it means that the company is generating "high quality" earnings. However, if the amount of cash is consistently less than net income, it is a warning that the company is having problems converting net income into cash.

2. It helps in identifying the way cash is flowing into and out of a company. A company that consistently generates more cash than it spends will be well-placed to increase dividends, lower its debts, or even acquire other companies.

Understanding Changes In Cash

Here are a few questions that will test your comprehension of cash flow:

• If John Smith invests some money into his startup, what effect does this have on the company's Cash account?

• When the company buys some inventory, what effect does this have on its Cash account?

• If the company gets a bank loan, how is the Cash account affected?

• When the company pays its Accounts Payable, how is the Cash account affected?

• If an asset like Land decreases, how does this affect the Cash account?

From the above questions, we can make the following assumptions:

• Whenever an asset (that isn't cash) increases, there is a reduction in the Cash account.

• Whenever an asset (that isn't cash) decreases, there is an increase in the Cash account.

• Whenever a liability increases, there is an increase in the Cash account.

• Whenever a liability decreases, there is a decrease in the Cash account.

• Whenever owner's equity increases, there is an increase in the Cash account.

• Whenever owner's equity decreases, there is a decrease in the Cash account.

Format Of A Cash Flow Statement

A cash flow statement is organized into the following four sections:

1. Operating activities

In this section, we convert the net income from accrual-based accounting to cash accounting. The accounts affected are those that fall under current assets and current liabilities, such as:

- Inventory

- Interest payable

- Accounts receivable

- Wages payable

- Income taxes payable

- Supplies

- Notes payable

- Payroll taxes payable

2. Investing activities

In this section, we report any purchase or sale of long-term and fixed assets. These include:

- Land

- Equipment

- Vehicles

- Buildings

- Furniture and fixtures

- Long-term investments

3. Financing activities

In this section, we report the repurchase or issuance of stocks and bonds, as well as payment of dividends. Financing activities tend to affect the following accounts:

- Bonds payable

- Preferred stock

- Retained earnings

- Notes payable

- Treasury stock

- Deferred income taxes

4. Supplemental information

Reporting non-cash transactions, interest paid on loans, and income taxes.

How The Balance Sheet Affects The Cash Flow Statement

In Chapter 4, you learned how a balance sheet is made up of different categories. You need to understand that any changes in these balance sheet categories will affect different sections of the cash flow statement. Here is a summary of where to record any balance sheet changes:

• A change in Current Assets (excluding cash) will be reported under Operating Activities.

• A change in Current Liabilities will be reported under
Operating Activities.

• A change in Long-Term Assets will be reported under Investing
Activities.

• A change in Long-term Liabilities will be reported under
Financing Activities.

• A change in Stockholder's Equity will be reported under
Financing Activities.

Preparing A Cash Flow Statement

Now that you have learned the theory behind the cash flow
statement, let's look an example. This example will include all
the three financial statements that you have learned so far.

John Smith loves to spend time on the internet buying and
selling different items. He decides to create a business out of his
passion for finding good deals online. On January 3rd, 2018,
John takes $1,500 of his own money and starts his business. He
calls the company Amazing Deals Co. On January 18, Amazing
Deals purchases 15 graphing calculators at $50 each. The
company doesn't engage in any other transaction for the month
of January.

On January 31, John prepares his financial statements:

Amazing Deals Co.
Income Statement
For the Month Ended January 31, 2018

Revenues	$0
Expenses	$0
Net Income	**$0**

AMAZING DEALS CO.
Balance Sheet as at 31st January, 2018

ASSETS		LIABILITIES	
Cash at Bank	$750	Liabilities	$0
Truck	$750	**Owner's Equity**	
		Capital – John Smith	$1,500
Total Assets	**$1,500**	**Total Liabilities and Equity**	**$1,500**

Amazing Deals Co.
Statement of Cash Flows
For the Month Ended January 31, 2018

Operating Activities

Net income	$0
Increase in inventory	$ (750)
Cash used in operating activities	$ (750)
Investing Activities	$0
Financing Activities	
Investment by owner	$1,500
Net increase in cash	$750
Cash at beginning of the month	$0
Cash at the end of the month	**$750**

According to Amazing Deal's income statement for January, there was neither any profit nor loss because there were no expenses or sales. But if you look at the cash flow statement, you will notice that the company's operating activities led to a decrease in cash by $750. This was the result of buying inventory worth $750 during January.

The investing activities section shows $0 while the financing activities section shows a $1,500 increase in cash due to the capital John invested in the business. Therefore, there is a positive net change of $750 in the Cash account. This can be verified using the balance sheet, which shows Cash at Bank to be $750 as of 31st January.

This simple example shows you the relationship between the three financial statements and how a transaction is recorded and verified.

Chapter Summary

Here are the key points of the chapter:

• A cash flow statement is a financial report that records all the cash generated and used by a company during a specific time interval. It is officially referred to as the statement of cash flows.

• The cash flow statement is used to determine how well net income is converted into cash. It is also used to identify the inflow and outflow of cash in a company.

• The cash flow statement is divided into four sections – operating activities, investing activities, financing activities, and supplemental information.

• A change in the Current Assets and Current Liabilities of a balance sheet will affect the Operating Activities section of the cash flow statement.

• A change in the Long-term Assets of a balance sheet will affect the Investing Activities section of the cash flow statement.

• A change in the Long-term Liabilities and Stakeholders' Assets of a balance sheet will affect the Financing Activities section of the cash flow statement.

In the next chapter, you will learn how basic financial ratios are used in accounting.

Chapter 7: Financial Ratios

In this chapter, you will learn some of the financial ratios that are used in accounting. You are going to learn the different classes of ratios before we move on to the key financial ratios. I am going to show you what each financial ratio means and how it is calculated. Since this is a beginner-level book, we are only going to focus on the basic financial ratios.

Classification Of Ratios

A ratio is defined as a numerical relation between two quantities. For example, if you have 500 bananas and 100 apples, the ratio of bananas to apples would be 500/100, which can be expressed either as 5:1 or simply 5.

In the same way, a financial ratio refers to the comparison between two pieces of financial information. Financial ratios can be grouped according to their general characteristics and their mode of construction. By construction, I am referring to the way a particular ratio is used to measure an aspect of a business.

For example, there are four ways of classifying ratios according to construction:

1. A coverage ratio – The measurement of a company's ability to meet its financial obligations.

2. A turnover ratio – The measurement of a company's gross benefit compared to the resources utilized.

3. A return ratio – The measurement of a company's net benefit compared to the resources utilized.

4. A component percentage – The ratio of one component of a product to the entire product.

By assessing the financial condition of a company, we can know whether it has the ability to meet its financial obligations. However, by assessing the operating performance of the company, we can determine whether it is utilizing its assets efficiently and profitably.

Types Of Financial Ratios

There are four main types of financial ratios that you need to know about at this level. Each one has several sub-categories:

• Liquidity ratios – Examples include current ratio, quick ratio, and cash ratio.

• Profitability ratios – Examples include the profit margin, return on assets, and return on equity.

• Activity ratios – Examples include inventory turnover, accounts receivables turnover, total assets turnover, and fixed assets turnover.

• Financial leverage ratios – Examples include debt to equity ratio, debt to assets ratio, and long-term debt to assets ratio.

Liquidity Ratios

These are ratios that provide information regarding a company's ability to meet its short-term debts. These short-term liabilities can only be paid off if the company is able to quickly convert some of its assets into cash. These assets are therefore referred to as liquid assets, and are usually recorded as current assets or working capital in financial statements. Working capital simply means the number of resources required to maintain daily operations in the company.

The general rule in accounting is that it's better to have a larger coverage of liquid assets to short-term liabilities. This sends the signal to investors that a company is able to pay its short-term debts and still finance its daily operations.

Let's look at three types of liquidity ratios:

1. Current ratio.

This ratio indicates the extent to which current liabilities are covered by current assets. It is used to determine whether a company's liquid assets (cash, inventory, marketable securities, etc) can readily pay off short-term liabilities (taxes, accrued expenses, etc). Its formula is as follows:

$$Current\ Ratio = \frac{Current\ Assets}{Current\ Liabilities}$$

The general rule is that the higher the current ratio, the better. However, under certain conditions, this assumption can be misleading, especially when you are comparing two different companies to invest in. The best thing to do would be to understand the types of current assets a company owns, and how fast it is able to convert them into cash to pay off its current liabilities.

2. Quick Ratio.

This refers to a company's ability to pay off short-term liabilities without being forced to sell its inventory. It is also known as the acid-test ratio. It is calculated using the following formula:

$$Quick\ Ratio = \frac{Current\ Assets - Inventory}{Current\ Liabilities}$$

Since the quick ratio doesn't factor in illiquid assets like inventory, it provides a more conservative estimate of a company's liquidity. If you compare the current ratio with the quick ratio and discover that the current ratio is considerably higher, then that is an indicator that the company is over-relying on its inventory to boost its current assets.

3. Cash ratio.

This is a measure of how much cash, and cash equivalents, there are in a company's current assets to pay off its current liabilities. It is usually calculated as follows:

$$Cash\ Ratio = \frac{Cash + Cash\ Equivalent + Invested\ Funds}{Current\ Liabilities}$$

This particular ratio is more stringent than the first two because it only focuses on the most liquid assets that any company can have on its books. It doesn't take into account assets like receivables or inventory because there is never any guarantee that these assets can be converted to cash fast enough to pay off current liabilities.

On the other hand, most financial reports do not use the cash ratio because it is unrealistic for a business to hold on to large cash reserves just in case some debts need to be paid. It is more profitable for the company to utilize the cash somehow to generate bigger returns.

Profitability Ratios

These ratios measure a company's ability to utilize resources to generate profit and increase shareholder value. Let's look at three types of profitability ratios:

1. Profit margin analysis.

Profit margin is defined as the amount of profit that a company generates as a percentage of its sales. The goal is to identify any positive or negative trends in the earnings of a company. A positive profit margin usually means a company is a good investment.

An income statement usually has four levels of profit. The two profit margins that we are interested in right now are the gross profit margin and operating profit margin. They are calculated as follows:

$$Gross\ Profit\ Margin = \frac{Gross\ Profit}{Net\ Sales\ (Revenue)}$$

$$Operating\ Profit\ Margin = \frac{Operating\ Profit}{Net\ Sales\ (Revenue)}$$

Gross profit margin is an indicator of the efficiency with which a company is using its resources to generate profits. Gross profit is calculated by subtracting the cost of goods sold (cost of sales) from the net sales.

Operating profit margin is an indicator of how well the management of a company is running operations. If investors want to know the decision-making competence of the managers, they will look at operating expenses such as sales, marketing, research and development, rental properties, and etc. Operating profit is calculated by subtracting operating expenses from the gross profit.

2. Return on assets.

This is a measure of the profitability of a company in relation to its total assets. This ratio indicates how efficiently management is utilizing the company's assets to generate profits. It is usually calculated as a percentage, and the higher the return, the greater the efficiency in asset utilization. The formula is shown below:

$$Return\ on\ Assets = \frac{Net\ Income}{Average\ Total\ Assets}$$

3. Return on equity.

This is a measure of the profitability of a company in relation to its shareholder equity. This ratio indicates the performance of a company's earnings and informs the shareholders how well their equity is being used by management. It is calculated using the formula below:

$$Return\ on\ Equity = \frac{Net\ Income}{Average\ Shareholders'\ Equity}$$

The return on equity is expressed as a percentage, and the higher the figure, the greater the efficiency of management in using the company's equity base.

Activity Ratios

These ratios are used to measure how well the assets in a company are being used to generate revenue. They help us assess the benefits generated by all the assets in a company or individual assets such as accounts receivable or inventory. For example, a company must be able to put its equipment to work to generate sales. This is why activity ratios are sometimes referred to as turnover ratios. The four types of activity ratios are:

1. Inventory turnover.

This is the ratio of a company's sales to its inventory. Inventory turnover can tell us whether a company has excess or insufficient inventory of finished goods. It is calculated as follows:

$$Inventory\ Turnover = \frac{Cost\ Of\ Goods\ Sold}{Inventory}$$

2. Accounts receivable turnover.

This is a ratio of the annual credit sales to annual accounts receivable. It is an indicator of the number of times a company has sold on credit and been paid for the goods or services. It is calculated using the formula below:

$$Accounts\ Receivable\ Turnover = \frac{Annual\ Credit\ Sales}{Accounts\ Receivable}$$

3. Total asset turnover.

This is simply the ratio of sales to total assets. It is a measure of the degree to which investment in assets leads to sales. It is calculated using the following formula:

$$Total\ Asset\ Turnover = \frac{Sales}{Total\ Assets}$$

If the total asset turnover is less than the industry average, it means that the company isn't generating enough volume of business relative to the size of its asset base.

4. Fixed asset turnover.

This is the ratio of sales to fixed assets. It is an indicator of the ability of a company to use its plant and equipment to generate sales. It is calculated using the formula:

$$Fixed\ Asset\ Turnover = \frac{Sales}{Fixed\ Assets}$$

Financial Leverage Ratios

When a company wants to finance its operations, it can do so through equity or debt. Using debt to finance a business is risky because the company becomes legally obligated to pay back the lenders the principal amount plus interest. This is not the case with equity financing because there is no legal obligation for the company to pay back the money to the shareholders. The board of directors can decide to release dividends or not.

When you look at how any company is operated, you will always see some level of business risk. However, the moment the company decides to finance its operations using a mix of equity and debt, another type of risk is added. This is known as financial risk. Financial risk is a measure of how much debt financing a company uses compared to equity financing.

Financial leverage ratios are an indicator of the level of financial risk taken on by a company. Let's look at three types of financial leverage ratios:

1. Total debt to assets ratio.

This ratio measures the extent to which a company has financed its assets using short-term and long-term debt. It is often referred to as debt ratio and is calculated using the formula:

$$Total\ Debt\ To\ Assets\ Ratio = \frac{Total\ Debt}{Total\ Assets}$$

If a company's debt to asset ratio is lower than the industry average, then it means that it is not too dependent on money borrowed from others. The higher the debt ratio, the greater the financial risk the company has taken on. However, big, well-established companies are able to maintain a high debt ratio without negatively affecting their balance sheet.

2. Debt to equity ratio

This ratio measures a company's total debt to its total shareholder equity. It is a comparison of how much creditors have pumped into the business versus the amount that shareholders have contributed. It is calculated using the formula:

$$Debt\ To\ Equity\ Ratio = \frac{Total\ Debt}{Total\ Shareholders'\ Equity}$$

Just like the debt to assets ratio, a lower debt to equity ratio is a good thing because it means the company has less debt compared to equity. It is important to note that both these ratios provide us with information about the capital structure of a company. Capital structure refers to the combination of debt and equity to finance assets.

3. Long-term debt to assets ratio.

This is the percentage of a company's total assets that are acquired using long-term debt. It is calculated using the formula:

$$Long-Term\ Debt\ to\ Assets\ Ratio = \frac{Long-Term\ Debt}{Total\ Assets}$$

These are just a few of the types of financial ratios that we have in accounting. The ones mentioned above will help you get started with your accounting practices, but as you progress into more technical areas, you will encounter many other ratios.

Chapter Summary

Here are the key points of the chapter:

• A ratio is a numerical relationship between two quantities. A financial ratio is a comparison between two pieces of financial information.

• Ratios can be classified according to coverage, turnover, returns, and component percentage.

• Liquidity ratios provide information regarding a company's ability to meet its short-term debts. Examples include current ratio, quick ratio, and cash ratio.

• Profitability ratios are used to measure a company's ability to utilize resources to generate profit and increase shareholder value. Examples include profit margin analysis, return on assets, and return on equity.

• Activity ratios are used to measure how well the assets in a company are being used to generate revenue. Examples include inventory turnover, accounts receivables turnover, fixed assets turnover, and total assets turnover.

• Financial leverage ratios are an indicator of the level of financial risk taken on by a company. Examples include debt to assets ratio, debt to equity ratio, and long-term debt to assets ratio.

Conclusion

Congratulations! You have reached the end of this accounting book. My goal was to help you establish a sound accounting foundation, and if you have been reading keenly, you should now be confident enough to handle many basic accounting functions. Accounting is considered to be a difficult subject to master by most people, but as you have learned, it's all about applying the knowledge you have as you go along.

The most important part of gaining accounting expertise is continuous practice. When you are learning about a particular concept, make sure you work out the examples and answer as many questions as possible on the topic. This is how you will gain the confidence to tackle more complex accounting functions.

You are now familiar with the basic structure of accounting. You have learned the functions of accounting and the importance of having accounting skills. There is no reason to be confused about the terminologies used in basic accounting, including the main differences between bookkeeping and accounting.

You have also learned about the two most important principles of bookkeeping concepts, i.e. the accounting equation and the double-entry rule. Remember that every transaction that you record and analyze must always comply with these two concepts.

I am honored that you took the time to read this book. I hope you enjoyed learning about accounting.

Thank you and good luck!

www.ingramcontent.com/pod-product-compliance
Lightning Source LLC
Chambersburg PA
CBHW061057050726
47592CB00004B/1710